"This is a perfect example of small things offering enormous impact. This is a book to read, to share and to give to all your managers!"

— JEANETTE K. WINTERS
Corporate Talent Management Executive
(Intel, American Express, Pitney Bowes & Amgen)

"Nuggets of management gold, applicable to aspiring managers and seasoned veterans alike."

— DAN RUBADO
Manager of Employee Engagement, On Trac Shipping

"If you are committed to the relentless pursuit of management concepts that are fundamental to successful outcomes, this book is a must."

— DAVID LIMARDI
Past President of The International City/County Management Association

*Just Plain
Good Management*

Robert B. Denhardt

JUST PLAIN GOOD MANAGEMENT
Robert B. Denhardt

All rights reserved. No part of this publication may be transmitted or reproduced in any media or form without the express consent of the author.

Copyright © 2014 Robert B. Denhardt

Published in the United States by New Insight Publishers, 1304 Normandy Ln., Sacramento, CA 95822

Just Plain Good Management
ISBN 978-0-9903938-0-1

Printed in the USA by MiniBük

Introduction

The ability to manage groups and organizations effectively and responsibly is one of the most important and most valued skills in society today. But good management is rare. If you think of the really good managers you have had in your career, the number will probably be small.

There are plenty of ways to manage poorly – and one of the most important is to fall victim to "theoretical overkill." Hundreds of faddish approaches to management are put forward each year by academics, consultants, and business writers. It's no wonder managers are often frustrated and confused by "theories" that don't match "practice."

Managing well is really not that hard. All that is required are a few simple ideas, practiced with patience, sincerity, and good will. In the following pages, you will learn dozens of common-sense lessons shared by the best managers in public, private, and nonprofit organizations in this country and around the world.

These lessons represent the core skills and ideas that guide good management today. They are not the lessons of the past, but those of today – the new management. The basic ideas aren't that difficult, but, if practiced consistently, they can make your organization more productive and your community a better place to live. And you and your people will likely feel happier and more engaged than ever before.

In any case, keep this book close to where you work so you can check occasionally to see if you are following these ideas. Take time daily or weekly to reflect on these lessons and make them part of who you are as a manager.

Here's the deal. It's simple. If you stand by these core skills and ideas, and if you do so consistently, you will not only be a good manager – you will be a great one!

Bob

The Lessons

Listen, Listen, Listen

The first and most important idea in good management is simple: listen, listen, listen. Failure to listen attentively, genuinely, thoughtfully, and completely is the cause of an incredible number of organizational breakdowns. On the other hand, listening carefully builds trust, engagement, and in turn, productivity. Practice not just hearing but really listening to others. Encourage people to listen to each other. And, who knows, people might even listen to you.

Nourish Creativity

You must plant the seeds of creativity in fertile soil. The best soil for growing great ideas is one that allows people to embrace uncertainty and ambiguity, to work together freely and without "ownership," and to communicate ideas where they will make a difference. Growing great ideas also benefits from the sunshine of encouragement from above. Guess what? You are both the gardener and the sunshine!

Maintain Balance in Your Life

Strive for a sense of balance in all that you do. Don't smoke. Drink only in moderation. Exercise regularly. Practice mindfulness. Remember that your work is only one part of your life. Don't forget the other parts. If you enjoy what you do at work, consider yourself lucky. If you don't enjoy what you do, consider doing something else. Management can be fun and challenging at the same time. There will be bad times – that's inescapable – but if you maintain a sense of balance, you'll get through the bad times and enjoy the good times even more.

Achieving Self-Awareness

For the last couple of thousand years, philosophers have pointed out that, in order to manage others, you must first learn to manage yourself. That's not easy. Indeed, it's often harder to manage yourself than others. First read, think, and talk with others about the skills and the qualities you associate with the best managers. Then spend serious time in self-reflection and self-critique – not beating yourself up – but being honest with yourself. Prepare yourself to reach your highest potential. In doing so, there's little you can do about your weaknesses, so identify and build on your strengths. That's where the real payoffs will come.

Relax

Being relaxed does not mean being unfocused. But don't be consumed by your work. In 99.99% of the cases you deal with, the world will not end based on your decision. Make time to get away. Learn what recharges your batteries and recharge occasionally. Take time to smell the roses, or whatever fragrance you prefer. Listen to good music, especially music that makes you dance. Taste the best cupcake you've ever had.

Maturity Helps

You can learn about management from books and blogs. That's cognitive. You can learn interpersonal skills from coaching, from well-conceived seminars, and from your own experience. But to do what you know in your head to be correct and to do what you have done successfully time after time, requires- self-esteem, self-confidence, and just plain maturity. That comes with age and experience, but it will happen more quickly if you engage in frequent self-reflection. And that doesn't mean that you should just stand in front of a mirror!

A Sense of Purpose

A vision is sometimes expressed as an end goal – what you want your organization to be when it grows up. However, that formulation may not be best for either you or your organization. First, you may quickly find that your vision doesn't fit what's happening around you – especially as you move through the weeks and months ahead. And, second, you need to be attentive to possible new directions in which you should move as things change around you. What you need instead is a sense of purpose – why does this organization exist? You need a clear, forward-looking direction to maintain the proper focus, but you also need excellent peripheral vision to see the opportunities as well as the challenges you encounter along the way.

Articulate Your Big Ideas

As a manager you will likely be presented with specific (or sometimes not very specific) goals to be accomplished. You may also have personal goals you want to achieve. In either case, it may be better to set your agenda in terms of big ideas or themes. Big ideas combine a sense of purpose and a focus or direction. Think of the big ideas that you want to guide your work and that of your organization. Your personal vision needs to express who you are and who you might become. Your organizational vision needs to do the same. Both need to be both realistic and forward-looking. Both need to address why you do what you do. They should be consistent; the values that guide your personal life should not be at odds with those that drive your work.

Theory Talks, But Practice Walks

You may state your values and those of the organization abstractly, but people will be watching to see what you actually do. If you are going to ask people to "Do as I say," you'd better be ready to do so yourself. Show them you are serious by walking the talk – and by praising and rewarding others who do the same. If you preach listening, listen. If you preach empathy, empathize. If you preach caring, care.

Know Your Stuff

You must be able to speak with knowledge and understanding both about the substance of your organization's work and about your approach to the management of the organization. But, importantly, if you don't know what you are talking about, don't fake it. Rather, admit that you don't know. Then start asking a lot of questions so that the next time someone asks, you'll know better than anyone else. It will also help to read this book!

Don't Over-Manage

Don't try to control people. Rather support what they do. Hire good people; give them the tools they need; and then get out of the way. It's tempting to micro-manage. Get over it. Micro-managing is a sign of excessive ego – and excessive ego is one of the main enemies of good management.

Learn From Failure

Hopefully, as you generate new ideas and undertake new programs, you and your employees will have many successes. However, inevitably you will have failures as well. Building a climate of openness and trust will help people understand that it's okay to fail – under two conditions: First, don't be glued to a failed idea. Put it aside. You must move on. Second, learn from your failure. Failure is one of the best teachers. But learning the lessons of failure is not always easy. And be sure you learn the right lessons.

Encourage Good Ideas

Always remember that while you may know a great deal about your field, you don't have a monopoly on good ideas. In fact, you don't even come close. As a manager, if you have three really good ideas a year, that's above average. But if you encourage all your people to bring forward three really good ideas each year, think how many you will have. That number will be way above average.

Dealing With Poor Performers

Everyone in the organization knows who the poor performers are, and, if they are not dealt with, everyone will resent that they are able to get away with it. Even worse, poor performance, if left unattended, is contagious. It's true – one bad apple can spoil the bunch. You have to take action, and that action should be measured and constructive rather than punitive. Ask whether they are willing and able. If they are willing but not able, try to provide what they need or help them develop their skills. If they are able but not willing, there's a motivation issue. See what you can do to help. But if someone is both unwilling and unable, it may be time to say good-bye. In any case, the process will take a lot of time and emotional energy. Everybody will be watching. But, in the long run, it's worth it, in terms of productivity, but also in terms of the trust and respect those watching will have for you.

Improving The Work

In the end, the people who do the work know the work best and know best how to improve the work. Recognize that, and recognize them.

Do The Right Thing

Every action you take will have ethical implications. So do the right thing. I repeat – do the right thing. If you don't know what the right thing is in a particular situation, talk with a trusted advisor – hopefully one outside your organization. Remember that being responsible may make you powerful, but being powerful won't ever make you responsible. It's hard enough to exercise power or influence ethically. Don't make it even harder. Finally, tell the truth – even when it hurts. Be honest with everyone – and especially with yourself. If you make a mistake, admit it and publicly work to correct it. That's the right thing to do.

Happiness Is Contagious

If you enjoy your work – and if you let that enjoyment show – others will likely follow your lead. While happy people are not always the most productive people, they usually are. And, even if they are not, they are a lot more fun to be around than a bunch of grouches. Laughter is still the best medicine.

Be Yourself

There's a lot of talk these days about being "authentic," but that's not a lot different from the traditional advice that you should be yourself. Pretending to be someone you are not will always get you in trouble. In contrast, sincerely expressing who you really are will build confidence and respect. Of course, that means you have to know who you are. It also means you must recognize that you are changing and evolving as a person and as a manager. That's good – especially if you are becoming your best self. Know yourself. Know who you are becoming. Be your best, and be yourself.

Be Humble, but Not Meek

As a manager, you will have to be active and assertive; you will have to make tough decisions and oversee their execution. You will be in a very public position – at least within your own organization. Under these conditions, you will be tempted to indulge your ego. Resist that temptation. Act with humility and modesty. But recognize that humility is not the same as meekness or submissiveness. Be proactive and assertive when you need to be. Meanwhile, take time to listen to others. Encourage their ideas. Show them respect. At the same time, build your own self-respect. Ego is bad. Confidence is good.

Challenge the Status Quo

Some people say that today you have to be comfortable with the uncomfortable: you can't let changes upset you. In a rapidly changing world, that's good advice. But think about the other side too. Maybe you should be uncomfortable with the comfortable. The normal way of doing things – the way we've always done it around here – is comfortable. But that very comfort should make you uncomfortable, because it's a sign someone is passing you by. Jazz trumpeter Miles Davis said, "If it sounds clean and slick, I've been doing it too long." You also should feel the urge to change, to move in a new direction. See the present not as where we have come, but a place to begin.

Handle Change With Care

So you recognize that things must change. But you know that change can be very upsetting for people – some who have good reasons to think the change won't work and others who simply are reacting negatively to the thought of doing things differently. The first group needs to be heard and educated; the second needs to be heard and reassured. More than anything else, both need for you to listen, listen, listen.

Say It Simply

It's a great skill to boil complex ideas down to their essence. That is not to say you should be simplistic. Indeed, taking difficult and complex ideas and distilling their essence is hard intellectual work. But communicating clearly and succinctly will help your people know where you are going and how they can help get the organization there. And be consistent – say the same thing in different settings and with different audiences. Don't oversimplify, but go to the essence. Keep your message clear, concise, and consistent.

Use Supportive Communications

Recognize that communication serves both to transmit information and to build relationships. In daily communications, make sure your communications focus on problems, not people. Make sure you are describing situations, not evaluating others. And be specific rather than general. There are exceptions, times when you must be evaluative, but make those the exceptions. And, in all cases, be attentive to the fact that your communications are affecting not only what people do, but how they feel – about you, about each other, and about the work.

Each Individual Is Different

In my view, the "science" of motivation is totally useless. It's an art. Remember that each individual is different, and that what motivates one won't necessarily motivate another. Remember also that what motivates you probably won't motivate someone else. (That's easy to forget.) Motivation is not mechanical; it's about people. Treat each person as an individual and get to know that individual. You can't actually motivate someone else, but you can provide the conditions and the atmosphere in which they will do their best work. Don't know what those are? Just ask!

It's All About Relationships

For the first six months of any new job and throughout every six months thereafter, make building relationships your top priority. Building relationships takes time – and sometimes feels like you are wasting time. You are not. Few things are more important.

Be Dependable

Don't promise what you can't deliver. But once you make a commitment, do what you say you will do. If you promise to look into a situation, look into it. If you promise a response, respond. If you need to keep a checklist of commitments, start it right away – then check off items as you do what you said. If you are dependable, people will not be surprised (or confused) by your actions. And if you keep them informed and up-to-date, they will not surprise you either.

Find a Mentor and a Champion

You will always benefit from open, honest, and confidential conversations with a mentor. Develop such a relationship with someone in your organization or a similar one, someone who will be willing to listen, help analyze your situation, and give good advice – which you can then follow or ignore. (After all, it's your life – and your career.) You should also develop a champion, someone well-placed in your organization or your industry who is willing to go to bat for you. After you have developed a mentor and a champion, give a little back by becoming a mentor or a champion for someone else.

Embrace Diversity

Those from diverse cultures and backgrounds represent a source of different ideas, different insights, and different skills. Diversity is not a problem waiting to be solved. It's a solution waiting to be found. Build on diversity and difference and you will see great benefits.

Be Fair

Nothing undermines a sense of engagement more than people feeling they are being treated unfairly. Low pay, poor working conditions, etc., can be tolerated (at least for a while). Being treated unfairly cannot.

Don't Squash Creativity

Avoid responding to new ideas from your people by saying things like: Yes, but… We've always done it that way. We can't do that. Or, the boss would never go along with that. Instead use phrases like: Yes, and…. Building on that…. How might we…? One manager said that when someone brings him an idea, even if he knows a way to improve it, he'll agree with the proposal as is. In his view, encouraging people to bring forward good ideas is more important than showing he knows a better way. Good advice.

Be Nice

The days of managers screaming and yelling are over. There's no longer any room for fear and intimidation in management. Very much to the contrary: care about people in your organization and let that caring show. Be compassionate and let that compassion show. Remember that there's no gain in hurting someone unnecessarily. In fact, in the end, it will likely come back to hurt you. It's the reverse Golden Rule: Others will usually do to you what you do to them.

Be Punctual

Being late, and especially being late all the time, sends the message that you don't respect others. Showing disrespect in any way will undermine everything you are trying to do. Be on time. And, by the way, when you are away, don't spend all your time on the phone with people back in the office. That also shows a lack of trust and respect. That's not what you want to communicate.

Conquer Your E-mail Addiction

Email and social media can be of great help in organizational communications. But they can also become addictive. Choose three times a day to check your email. Read what's there, then, before you even answer the first, revisit your to-do list for the day. If it hasn't changed based on what you just read, wait until the end of the day to respond. Or just hit "delete."

Act Immediately – or Not

Consider carefully the timing of your responses to problems that arise, whether technical or people problems. In some cases, it's important to act quickly, to nip the problem in the bud, to be decisive. But in other cases taking time to think through the issue – or even just waiting for things to play out a little further – is best. Be attentive to timing and you will begin to learn the right moment to act.

Take the High Road

While you may see others get ahead by playing politics, that's not a good long-term strategy. Politics is driven by ego, and ego is incompatible with good management. Do your work carefully, responsibly, and effectively, and advances will come. Even if they don't, you will know that you have taken the high road ... and you will sleep better than anyone else.

Recognize the Whole Person

Respect the home and family life of your people. Try not to intrude on their private time or space. Don't create after hours emergencies out of nothing. Remember that what people do after work can enrich their work life. And respecting your people's personal life is just the right thing to do.

Forgive and Forget

Everyone is entitled to at least one screw-up a year. Try to help your employees understand what happened, then forgive and forget. And treat yourself in the same way. Allow yourself one screw-up a year. Where that happens, take responsibility and apologize. You'll probably survive. But, if your screw-ups begin to pile up, pack your bags. You're going away.

Be Visible

Don't isolate yourself. Your people will always feel some distance between you and them. And they will attribute that to poor communications. That's natural and inevitable. Don't do anything at all to make it worse. If you spend long periods away from the office, let people know what you are doing. When you are there, talk with people. And talk about what they want to talk about, even if it's not business. Smile. Be friendly. Not only will you build trust and good will, you are likely to learn more than you ever thought possible.

Know the History

Know the history of the organization, but don't be bound by it. Many practices that seem peculiar and even inefficient today made perfectly good sense when they were developed and implemented decades ago. Knowing how the organization came about and the circumstances under which it grew up can give you great insights into how to understand and frame possible changes in the organization.

Dealing With Jerks

Every organization with more than five managers has at least one manager who is a jerk. Every organization that has more than ten people has at least one employee who is a jerk. Most jerks don't recognize who they are, but they can be very disruptive (and not in a good way). But remember that you may too easily label someone a jerk who is disgruntled for good reason. Meet them head-on: Learn the source of their anger and, if possible, do something about it. Recovering jerks can actually become your strongest allies. And, incidentally, if you are in a meeting with four other managers and don't recognize the jerk at the table, maybe it's time for a little self-examination.

Calm Down, Then Act

Don't make important decisions when you are distracted or under extreme stress. For example, don't fire someone the day you return from vacation. Wait until you get a grasp on the current situation and carefully formulate your plan of action. Similarly, don't respond immediately to an e-mail that angers you. Take time to calm down. Draft a response and put it away for a few hours. Then try again. Abraham Lincoln apparently had a drawer full of heated letters he drafted then reconsidered. That's not a bad model.

Conflict Happens

Like most people, you are probably fearful of conflict – mostly because you grew up associating conflict with anger and fighting. And, indeed, conflict based on ego can be highly destructive. But conflict based on ideas can be quite healthy. It provides an opportunity for thoughts to be developed, to be tested, and to be either dismissed or confirmed. And that's a good thing. Your main job here is to create conditions where people are comfortable disagreeing about ideas and proposals – even disagreeing with you – without being disagreeable. You won't learn much from those who agree with you. You'll learn a lot from those who don't.

Use the Right Channel

There are many ways to communicate these days – personal conversation, e-mail and texting, video conferencing. Some are better in one situation, others are better in another. For example, e-mail can go quickly to many people at once, but doesn't allow the possibility of immediate response and clarification that you get in person-to-person conversations. Think carefully about the advantages of one channel rather than another and choose the one that best accomplishes what you want.

Handle Teams With Care

Effective teams can do marvelous things, but they require a great deal of care. First don't create a team just because you don't know what else to do. But if you form a team, be sure the right people are on it, people who can play nicely with others even though they differ (as you actually hope they will). Be clear about what you expect from the team, and be careful not to do its work yourself. Do whatever you can to reduce the dynamics of power on the team – power works directly in opposition to collaboration. And, in any case, don't expect miracles. But be grateful for positive results. And celebrate the success of the team at every possible occasion.

Reward Good Efforts, Not Just Good Results

Sometimes people with the best intentions can't complete a particular job. But if they have given their very best, recognize and reward that effort. Then provide the tools, the ideas, the training, and the help they need to get the job done. If you acknowledge and reward their effort, they will make that same effort again. If you don't, they won't.

The Smartest Person in The Room

Sometimes managers or others think they are the smartest person in the room. It's difficult to be the smartest person in the room. What should you do? First, be sure you are. Don't confuse smart with ego. Are you as smart as you think you are? Second, recognize that smart can be intimidating and that intimidation undermines teamwork. Third, smart needs to be balanced by common-sense. Fourth, smart isn't always the most effective in the long run. Building relationships is usually much more important than being smart.

Understand the Rhythms of Your Organization

Individuals have both physiological and psychological rhythms (your heartbeat, the way you swing your arms when you walk, the pace of your work). Groups and organizations also have rhythms. Think about what happens when a new boss comes in with a rhythm that is completely different from the established rhythm in an organization. It's chaos and highly destructive. Understanding the rhythms of your organization and understanding the way you affect those rhythms will give you an extra insight into what's going on around you. Feel the beat. Help your people dance.

Protect and Defend

One thing your people will appreciate most is your protecting them from the madness swirling above and around your group. You need to communicate what's going on, but there's no need to overstate it, nor to panic. Absorb some of the madness yourself, so it doesn't interfere with your people's work. You must also be an advocate for your group and a defender of those in it. Stand up for them when they are being abused from above or outside. Don't let the surrounding organizational "noise" drive your people crazy. You have the capacity to dial it down.

Resilience and Adaptability

You can expect the unexpected. Things will happen every day that will surprise and amuse or annoy you. Some "crisis" thing will happen every week that will distress or alarm you. Both you and your organization must be ready to face the unexpected and respond effectively. You can build that capacity – but not through rational planning, because you can't plan for surprises. Boxer Joe Louis said, "Everyone has a plan – until you get hit!" But the more you deal with uncertainty and ambiguity and adaptability in small doses from day to day, the better you will be able to deal with the bigger crisis when it hits. Through experience, you can build a capacity for resilience, both personally and organizationally. Combine resilience with an adaptive management style and you'll be in good shape when the unexpected shows up to try to ruin your day.

Make Change Work for You

We used to think of change as a hiccup in the normal state of stability. Now stability is a hiccup in the normal state of change. To succeed in this new environment you must make adjustments. First, you must learn to be accepting of change. Life is change. Management is change. Get used to it. Second, you must be able to go with the flow of change, then move it in line with your intent. Don't let change throw you off your game. Learn to embrace change as an opportunity, then capitalize on this opportunity. Think carefully about how to make change work for you. Change will happen. Whether it helps or hurts is up to you. Finally, by yourself, you can only nudge change in the right direction. But if you involve lots of people in the change process, the nudge can turn into a real push.

The Foundational Skills

We used to contrast the technical skills (the manual and mechanical skills required for the job) with the people skills (skills such as communications, motivation, and interpersonal relations). We soon came to recognize that people skills are just as important as technical skills, if not even more so. But the new management recognizes still another set of skills or qualities: empathy, humility, generosity, balance, patience, self-awareness, learning agility, caring and compassion. And what we are now learning is that these skills and qualities are as important as the other skills, even more so. Indeed, they are foundational. This is not where you end up. This is where you start.

Learning in the New World

It's a new world. Hierarchy is a relic. Top-down is history. The word "boss" is an anachronism. In the new management, the old skills of structure, control, and rational planning just won't work. The management capabilities of the coming decades will include flexibility, adaptability, agility, resilience, negotiation, compromise, conflict resolution, and collaboration. Look for ways to learn these capabilities. You must engage in constant education and reeducation. But choose carefully. Don't settle for books or educational programs that teach the same old thing. Demand more and make sure you get it.

Transformation

To be the best manager you can be, you must regularly transform yourself. Everything around you is changing and you have to change too. Today we are moving to greater autonomy and adaptability in the workplace. Managers frozen in the styles of the past won't be able to keep up with the new world these ideas present. In any case, management is not situational, changing from organization to organization, as we once thought. Today managers have to adapt to the times and spaces in which we live, not to particular kinds of organizations. Do everything you can to understand the culture around you. Read the best books, recite great poetry, watch the best movies, listen to the best music, study art and architecture, and tune into the currents of heroism and adventure in your time. Study the lives of your cultural heroes. They may provide lessons in how to adapt to and move your world.

Management and Leadership

If you have gotten this far, you are serious about being a better manager, a good or even great manager. But how about the next step – becoming a leader. We need leaders throughout our groups, our organizations, and our society. You can develop your leadership skills and those of others by practice, reflection, and experimentation. Leadership today doesn't mean setting a vision or goal then forcing people in that direction. It means working with your group or organization to identify people's commitments and their preferences, articulating the resulting direction, and then triggering movement in that direction.

Empathy

Remember the first lesson of management: listen, listen, listen. Assuming you've got that down, now give it a twist. Listen empathetically. Try to pick up the tiny nuances of sound and movement that give away what's really happening inside a person. Walk a mile in their shoes, even if their shoes don't quite fit and are the wrong color. Empathy is the watchword of the new management. Sympathize, empathize – but then take the next step. Be responsive to the needs and desires of others. Empathy provides the entrée to caring and compassion, and caring and compassion provide the entrée to love. Ultimately, management should be deeply rooted in empathy, caring, compassion, and love.

Other Books by Robert B. Denhardt

In the Shadow of Organization

The Pursuit of Significance

The Dance of Leadership
(with Janet Denhardt)

Theories of Public Organization
(with Thomas Catlaw)

The New Public Service
(with Janet Denhardt)

Volume Orders

You can receive substantial discounts on volume orders of *Just Plain Good Management* (500 copies and above).

For further information and to place an order, please email:

orderJPGM@gmail.com

or call **916-942-9160.**